Quotes and Scripture on Prayer

This book is dedicated to my parents Bishop Emeritus George K. Tibeesigwa and Mrs. Efrance Tibeesigwa. You showed me the way, you taught me that prayer is what will keep me afloat through life.

To every child of God that longs for intimacy with the Father and fuel to walk life's journey.

Quotes and Scripture on Prayer

The greatest privilege God gives to you is the freedom
to approach Him at any time

- Wesley L. Duewel

RACHEL A. BAALESSANVU

"The greatest privilege God gives to you is the freedom to approach Him at any time. You are not only authorized to speak to Him; you are invited. You are not only permitted; you are expected. God waits for you to communicate with Him. You have instant, direct access to God".

~ Wesley L. Duewel

"Rachel is a passionate and valiant prayer warrior, who leads our teams here at Worship Harvest Naalya in corporate prayer weekly before the services. She is helping us build a culture of both personal and corporate prayer among the leaders. She has put together a wonderful resource to help rekindle any heart with a fire that burns for the presence of God and the things of God. I highly recommend it for everyone. It's a wonderful read."

Moses Mukisa

Senior Pastor, Worship Harvest Ministries

Kampala, Uganda

The beauty of prayer is found in its simplicity. Conversation between a child and their loving parent. Rachel wonderfully shares this throughout the book, graciously bringing you along and inspiring conversation between you and a loving Heavenly Father.

Charity Kwatampora

Pastor, Worship Harvest Jinja

Jinja, Uganda

Rachel is so passionate about God and understands that prayer is the heartbeat of God. When the Holy Spirit dropped the idea of having prayer sessions before Sunday service begins at Worship Harvest Ministries, I knew she was pregnant for this and it was time to birth and support this ministry because of the overwhelming hunger she had for this altar to be established. Rachel is a prayer warrior and knows exactly what to do in time of battle.

When overwhelmed by circumstances and you walk to Rachel, she will simply show you that the first solution to any challenge is Prayer but above all encourage you to pray in the spirit.

Over the years, I have learnt that Prayer has no limitations. Do not make it so complicated. Pray at all times and from anywhere. When you choose to make prayer bread and butter that is when you will appreciate that it is your daily bread. These quotes and scripture will unlock lots of things that you took for granted about prayer. Be blessed as you get ministered to.

Rebecca Amoding

Head of Human Resources, Uniliver Uganda Ltd

Kampala, Uganda

Being the engineer she is, Rachel presents to us her thoughts on prayer in a precise and straight to the point manner. And yet, it is clear that this book has been born out of deep places. My favourite part is the reference scriptures for the different

Rachel puts together the best guide that a number of renowned authors, speakers, prayer warriors, biblical authorities including theologians and spiritual leaders have to say about Prayer. This product together with thematic scripture makes this piece a worthwhile must read.

I am extremely encouraged, challenged and invited to pray the more. I lovingly and passionately encourage and invite you to read this piece and pray more. You will not regret. Thank you Rachel.

Bishop Dr. George William K. Tibeesigwa
Vice Chancellor, VUST, Bushenyi, Uganda
Retired Bishop of Ankole Diocese, Mbarara, Uganda
Father of the Author

Table of Contents

The subject of prayer is as enigmatic as they come. Commonly understood as the conversation one has with a higher deity to "ask" for blessings, protection, favor, luck... the shopping list goes on.

Our common understanding is also embedded in our vernacular rendering of the word. In most Bantu languages it is directly translated as to "ask".

This couldn't be further from the truth.

Those that have ventured deeper into prayer have discovered a hidden power, a fountain of wisdom and an intimate place of communion with our Father.

Rachel has ventured on this journey for as long as I have known her. Passionate about prayer, she isn't satisfied with the surface touch and go where we whisper common words we learned back in Sunday school as we sleep off, or the "God help me" screams that we shout when all is not going as we want. She hungers for more; for a deeper, further, closer intimacy with our Creator. Having known her for the better part of 17 years, I have come to appreciate this hunger. I have had a front row seat watching her hunger translate to action then to passion. To watch the intercessor in her get energized and manifest.

This book won't give you tips to improve your prayer life or keys to get the most out of God. It simply ignites your passion for this close space by sharing a collection of other likeminded spiritual deep swimmers. As each quote narrates the heart of the author, you get a sense of connection to what they are experiencing. Rachel knits these words with biblical references and adds to that her experiences with these scriptures.

This book will amaze you, inspire you, convict you, reaffirm you and challenge you. Like prayer itself, its simplicity is its power.

Looking back at my own Christian walk, much of my dysfunction with prayer was due to the complexity in which it was painted to me. Too many dos and don'ts before you are let in to talk to God. For a process that was supposed to be refreshing and rejuvenating, it sure was hard and stressful to do. I relate with many who feel this way; many who have been sold a gospel of works and deeds. We have portrayed God as a moody, demanding, angry, jealous man ready to throw a bolt of lightning at you at the slightest hint of sin. No wonder we have a disillusioned Christian walk.

This book brings out the beauty and simplicity of prayer. It is a tapestry of well-articulated thoughts, carefully research scriptural references and hearty honest conversation with the author.

Quotes and Scriptures on Prayer is a girl's story about conversations with her Father and she brings along other world renown authors on this journey of discovery of this wonderful gift we call PRAYER.

~Noah Baalessanvu

Are you weary of a mundane and powerless prayer life? Are you asking *why pray anyway?* This book of quotes and scriptures on prayer has been put together to start you on a journey of discovery in prayer.

Discover who God is and who you are in Christ Jesus. Other saints are walking this same journey and have shared their experiences with us. May this booklet ignite an unquenchable thirst in you to have your own experience in prayer.

Together, we shall touch heaven and change earth through prayer.

~Rachel A. Baalessanvu

Do you know what prayer is?
Do you know why you need to pray?
Do you know how to pray?

Many are the thoughts and experiences surrounding the subject of prayer. Prayer has been considered a duty, hard work, uninteresting, even religious.

I consider prayer to be the greatest privilege I have as a believer. Wesley Duewel couldn't have said it any better. He says "The greatest privilege God gives to you is the freedom to approach Him at any time. You are not only authorized to speak to Him; you are invited. You are not only permitted; you are expected. God waits for you to communicate with Him. You have instant, direct access to God."

In this book, I have put together quotes on prayer that I relate to my own journey of prayer including learning how to pray. When I read them, they remind me of the vastness of the character of God and the uniqueness of the relationship we each have with Him. As a child of God, you can hone in on this special privilege of relating with the beauty of a loving Father; a Father who comes to us, reveals himself to us, lets us in on His heart and allows us to partner with him. We do this in prayer.

As you start on or continue on a journey of prayer, may the experience of others in prayer be a glimpse into the greatness you are going to experience on your own journey.
The icing on the cake are the scriptures from the Bible on the subject of prayer. Prayer was God's idea allowing the beauty and splendor of heaven to touch earth.
Come and dine. God is expecting you.

Prayer is the greatest privilege we have that allows us to commune and relate with the creator of the universe ~Rachel A. Baalessanvu.

Hello dad!
Help!!!!!!
I love you!
I need you!
What do you think?
Please help him!
Thank you!
I am sorry!
Yes Lord!
I'll do it!
That is prayer.
Simply talking to God about any and everything.

"Is prayer your steering wheel or your spare tire?"

~ *Corrie ten Boom*

"Prayer is not to remind God what your problems are, but prayer is to remind your problems who God is."

~*Unknown*

"Prayer is not monologues, but dialogue; God's voice is its most essential part. Listening to God's voice is the secret of the assurance that He will listen to mine."

~ *Andrew Murray*

"Prayer is not overcoming God's reluctance. It is laying hold of His willingness."

~*Juliana of Norwich*

"Prayer is simply talking to God like a friend and should be the easiest thing we do each day."

~*Joyce Meyer*

"Prayer is not asking. Prayer is putting oneself in the hands of God, at His disposition, and listening to His voice in the depth of our hearts."

~Mother Teresa

"Prayer is man giving God the legal right and permission to interfere in earth's affairs."

~Unknown

"Prayer is the key that unlocks all doors."

~Unknown

"True prayer is measured by weight, not by length. A single groan before God may have more fullness of prayer in it than a fine oration of great length."

~ C. H. Spurgeon

"Prayer is the link that connects us with God."

~Unknown

"Prayer is not learned in a classroom but in the closet."

~E. M. Bounds

"Prayer is also an act of obedience. We are exhorted to pray for others and to pray without ceasing."

~Robin Jones Gunn

"Prayer is not a check request asking for things from God. It is a deposit slip – a way of depositing God's character into our bankrupt souls."

~ Dutch Sheets

"Prayer is not a discourse. It is a form of life, the life with God. That is why it is not confined to the moment of verbal statement."

~Jaques Ellul

"Prayer is not so much an act as it is an attitude — an attitude of dependency, dependency upon God."

~Arthur Pink

"Prayer is the master strategy that God gives for the defeat and rout of Satan."

~Wesley L. Duewel

"Prayer is the supreme way to be workers together with God."

~Wesley L. Duewel

"Prayer is the exercise of drawing on the grace of God."

~Oswald Chambers

"Prayer at its highest is a two-way conversation, and for me, the most important part is listening to God's replies."

~Frank C. Laubach

"Prayer is God's ordained way to bring His miracle power to bear in human need."

~Wesley L. Duewel

"Prayer lays hold of God's plan and becomes the link between His will and its accomplishment on earth. Amazing things happen, and we are given the privilege of being the channels of the Holy Spirit's prayer."

~ Elisabeth Elliot

Prayer is a means of capturing the heartbeat of heaven, partnering with God and hosting heaven's agenda on earth. ~ Rachel A. Baalessanvu

We have been given all. Christ died once for all and through His death we won ourselves a complete package that includes salvation, health, provision, relationship, victory, deliverance, wisdom, knowledge, understanding, name it. Through prayer we have access to all and more.

"As His divine power has given to us all things that pertain to life and godliness, through the knowledge of Him who called us by glory and virtue," **2Peter 1:3 (NKJV)**

"The battle you fight today will be your victory in God tomorrow."

~Cindy Jacobs

"Our intercession rises as incense."

~Unknown

"Prayer reaches in the unseen, to the very throne room of God, to procure miracles for impossible solutions."

~Jennifer Eivaz

"Prayer is an absolute necessity to the proper carrying on of God's work."

~E.M. Bounds

"He who kneels the most, stands the best."

~Dwight L. Moody

"To get nations back on their feet, we must first get down on our knees."

~ Billy Graham

"There are parts of our calling, works of the Holy Spirit, and defeats of the darkness that will come no other way than through furious, fervent, faith-filled, unceasing prayer."

~Beth Moore

"The reality is, my prayers don't change God. But, I am convinced prayer changes me. Praying boldly boots me out of that stale place of religious habit into authentic connection with God Himself."

~Lysa TerKeurst

"Time spent in prayer is not time wasted but time invested."

~Myles Munroe

"There is nothing that makes us love a man so much as praying for him."

~William Law

"We must begin to believe that God, in the mystery of prayer, has entrusted us with a force that can move the Heavenly world, and can bring its power down to earth."

~Andrew Murray

"Nothing tends more to cement the hearts of Christians than praying together. Never do they love one another so well as when they witness the outpouring of each other's hearts in prayer."

~ Charles Finney

"God never gives us discernment in order that we may criticize, but that we may intercede."

~ Oswald Chambers

"If your day is hemmed in with prayer, it is less likely to come unraveled."

~Cynthia Lewis

"The amount of time we spend with Jesus, meditating on His Word and His majesty, seeking His face, establishes our fruitfulness in the kingdom."

~Charles Stanley

"The greatest gift we can give to others is our prayers."

~ Unknown

"We can be tired, weary, and emotionally distraught, but after spending time alone with God, we find that He injects into our bodies energy, power and strength."

~Charles Stanley

"When my arms can't reach people who are close to my heart, I always hug them with my prayers."

~Unknown

"Prayer is striking the winning blow at the concealed enemy. Service is gathering up the results of that blow among the men we see and touch."

~Samuel Gordon

"Have you ever learned the beautiful art of letting God take care of you and giving all your thought and strength to pray for others and for the kingdom of God? It will relieve you of a thousand cares."

~A. B. Simpson

My words are not idle. My thoughts are not stray. When I pray, my response is to act on what I have heard. I pay attention to that thought and I speak it out or act it out.
~ Rachel A. Baalessanvu

When we pray, God's response to us is one that says, "Welcome my child, I have been expecting you."
God listens to us, talks to us, asks some things of us, affirms us, loves on us, commissions us, encourages us, and corrects us. Our prayer allows God to intervene in our everyday lives. When we ask for particular things, He answers or in His wisdom withholds a particular answer.

When we pray, our response or posture should be one of listening, praise and worship to our God, gratitude, full abandonment, OBEDIENCE, focusing on God and not our situation. Our prayers should leave us, and those we pray for, better people.

"When you pray, you should, (P)our out your heart, (R)ealize God will answer, (A)lways believe , (Y)ield to what God tells you."

~Unknown

"Don't let the absence of an immediate breakthrough change your revelation of God's nature."

~ Unknown

"Get on your knees and ask for the blessings of the Lord, then stand on your feet and do what you are asked to do."

~Gordon B Hinckley

"Prayer should not be regarded as a duty which must be performed, but rather as a privilege to be enjoyed, a rare delight that is always revealing some new beauty."

~ E.M. Bounds

"If you want that splendid power in prayer, you must remain in loving, living, lasting, conscious, practical, abiding union with the Lord Jesus Christ."

~ C. H. Spurgeon

" When God speaks, oftentimes His voice will call for an act of courage on our part."

~Charles Stanley

"We never know how God will answer our prayers, but we can expect that He will get us involved in His plan for the answer. If we are true intercessors, we must be ready to take part in God's work on behalf of the people for whom we pray."

~Corrie ten Boom

"Always respond to every impulse to pray. The impulse to pray may come when you are reading or when you are battling with a text. I would make an absolute law of this: always obey such an impulse."

~Martyn Lloyd-Jones

"Any concern too small to be turned into a prayer is too small to be made into a burden."

~ Corrie Ten Boom

"We lie to God in prayer if we do not rely on him afterwards."

~ Robert Leighton

"Some prayers are followed by silence because they are wrong, others because they are bigger than we can understand."

~Oswald Chambers

"Have you ever thought what a wonderful privilege it is that every one each day and each hour of the day has the liberty of asking God to meet him in the inner chamber and to hear what He has to say?"

~Andrew Murray

"God always answers our prayer. Either He changes the circumstances, or he supplies sufficient power to overcome them."

~Unknown

"I have had prayers answered–most strangely so sometimes–but I think our heavenly Father's loving kindness has been even more evident in what He has refused me.”

~ *Lewis Carroll*

“Every time we pray our horizon is altered, our attitude to things is altered, not sometimes, but every time, and the amazing thing is that we don’t pray more.”

~ *Oswald Chambers*

“God never denied that soul anything that went as far as heaven to ask it.”

~*John Trapp*

“God does not stand afar off as I struggle to speak. He cares enough to listen with more than casual attention. He translates my scrubby words and hears what is truly inside. He hears my sighs and uncertain groping as fine prose.”

~ *Timothy Jones*

“Avail yourself of the greatest privilege [*prayer*] this side of heaven. Jesus Christ died to make this communion and communication with the Father possible.”

~*Billy Graham*

In prayer you're as vulnerable as a babe, yet you stand strong. You have constant access to the Father, wielding the power of the full Godhead. Nothing is impossible.
~Rachel A. Baalessanvu

The power of prayer is not a subject of you and I; it is not words we say or the way we say them or even how often we say them. The power of prayer is not based on the physical positioning of our bodies or use of artifacts. The power of prayer comes from the All-powerful One who hears our prayers and answers them. Prayer places us in contact with the Almighty God, and we should expect results, whether or not His choice answer is yes or no. Whatever the answer to our prayers, the God to whom we pray is the source of the power of prayer.

"The wonderful thing about prayer is that you leave a world of not being able to do something, and enter God's realm where everything is possible."

~ Corrie ten boom

"Prayer and sinning will never live together in the same heart. Prayer will consume sin, or sin will choke prayer."

~J. C. Ryle

"The one concern of the devil is to keep Christians from praying. He fears nothing from prayerless studies, prayerless work, and prayerless religion. He laughs at our toil, mocks at our wisdom, but trembles when we pray."

~Samuel Chadwick

"Our prayers may be awkward. Our attempts may be feeble. But since the power of prayer is in the one who hears it and not in the one who says it, our prayers do make a difference."

~Max Lucado

"Prayer does not change God, but it changes him who prays."

~ Soren Kierkegaard

"God shapes the world by prayer. The more praying there is in the world the better the world will be, the mightier the forces against evil."

~ *Mother Teresa*

"The most awesome power every human being possesses: the power to influence earth from heaven through prayer."

~*Myles Munroe*

"The more you pray, the less you'll panic. The more you worship, the less you'll worry. You'll feel more patient and less pressured."

~*Rick Warren*

"When the devil sees a man or woman who really believes in prayer, who knows how to pray, and who really does pray, and, above all, when he sees a whole church on its face before God in prayer, he trembles as much as he ever did, for he knows that his day in that church or community is at an end."

~*R.A. Torrey*

"When we pray, we relax, reflect, and renew our commitments to God. The peace that comes from consulting with God and receiving His divine wisdom is a powerful hug."

~David DeNotaris

"The power of our prayers, lies not primarily in our effort and striving, or in any technique, but rather in our knowledge of God."

~ Timothy Keller

"All I know is that when I pray, coincidences happen; and when I don't pray, they don't happen."

~Dan Hayes

"If you are a stranger to prayer, you are a stranger to the greatest source of power known to human beings."

~ Bill Sunday

"I remember my mother's prayers and they have always followed me. They have clung to me all my life."

~Abraham Lincoln

"Fight all your battles on your knees and you win every time."

~Charles Stanley

"I have often learned much more in one prayer than I have been able to glean from much reading and reflection."

~Martin Luther

"Our prayers lay the track down on which God's power can come. Like a mighty locomotive, His power is irresistible, but it cannot reach us without rails."

~Watchman Nee

"Prayer is the slender nerve that moves the muscle of Omnipotence".

~J. Edwin Hartill

"Nothing lies beyond the reach of prayer except that which lies outside the will of God."   ~Unknown

"The best reason to pray is that God is really there. In praying, our unbelief starts to melt. God moves smack into the middle of even an ordinary day."

~Emily Griffin

"How far away is heaven? It is not so far as some imagine. It wasn't very far for Daniel. It was not so far off that Elijah's prayer, and those of others, could not be heard there. Men full of the Spirit can look right into heaven."

~Dwight L. Moody

Every time I feel the Spirit moving in my heart, I will pray. And when in doubt, I will pray the Word of God.
~Rachel A. Baalessanvu

How does one answer the question, "How should I pray?" without sounding religious?

I have learnt that for me to pray right I need to pray God's heart for someone or for a situation. Many a time I have gone to God with my own requests and yes, there is a place for that, but I have learnt to go to God and listen in on what is on His heart at that moment. Sometimes all I need is to stay quiet, other times I need to pour my love on God, other times I need to battle in prayer. I'll start one way and end up in a totally different direction.

Whatever the case, I would say whenever you pray, pray believing that God hears you, take the focus off of you and place it on God. Listen, and pray God's heart. Pray His word.

"When we pray from a place of peace and not fear, we will see fruit."

~ Beni Johnson

"If you believe in prayer at all, expect God to hear you. If you do not expect, you will not have. God will not hear you unless you believe He will hear you; but if you believe He will, He will be as good as your faith."

~ Charles Spurgeon

"Rather than set aside daily time for prayer, I pray constantly and spontaneously about everything I encounter on a daily basis. When someone shares something with me, I'll often simply say, 'let's pray about this right now."

~ Thomas Kinkade

"God speaks in the silence of the heart. Listening is the beginning of prayer."

~ Mother Teresa

"The word of God is the food by which prayer is nourished and made strong."

~ E. M. Bounds

"To have God speak to the heart is a majestic experience, an experience that people may miss if they monopolize the conversation and never pause to hear God's responses."

~Charles Stanley

"Pray in Humility, in Faith, in accordance with God's Will, Others-focused, in the name of Jesus."

~ Unknown

"When I don't really know what to pray or how to pray, I take God's words and make them my prayers."

~Dannah Gresh

"There is a mighty lot of difference between saying prayers and praying."

~John G. Lake

"You may pray for an hour and still not pray. You may meet God for a moment and then be in touch with Him all day."

~Fredrik Wisloff

"All you need to do to learn to pray is to pray."

~ Wesley L. Duewel

"Prayer can never be in excess."

~C. H. Spurgeon

"Praying in faith is not an inner conviction that God will act according to our desires if only we believe hard enough. It involves believing that God will always respond to our prayers in accord with His nature, His purposes, and His promises."

~ Alvin VanderGriend

"To pray rightly, you must make God your hope, stay, and all. Right prayer sees nothing substantial or worth being concerned about except God."

~John Bunyan

"Prayers prayed in the Spirit never die until they accomplish God's intended purpose. His answer may not be what we expected, or when we expected it, but God often provides much more abundantly than we could think or ask. He interprets our intent and either answers or stores up our prayers. Sincere prayers are never lost. Energy, time, love, and longing can be endowments that will never be wasted or go unrewarded."

~ Wesley L. Duewel

"Pray the largest prayers. You cannot think a prayer so large that God, in answering it, will not wish you had made it larger. Pray not for crutches but for wings."

~ Phillips Brooks

"God knows what's in our hearts. We might as well get right to the point."

~ Bruce Bickel

"Stop praying for things and start praying for people."

~ Bret Nicholaus

"The call to unceasing prayer is not an invitation to divided consciousness; it does not imply that we pay any less attention to daily realities or retreat from life's responsibilities. It means being consciously, constantly conscious of the presence of God amidst the changing complexion of everyday life."

~ Debra Farrington

"Beware in your prayer, above everything, of limiting God-not only by unbelief, but by fancying that you know what He can do."

~Andrew Murray

"Groanings which cannot be uttered are often prayers which cannot be refused."

~ Charles Spurgeon

"Since you are tempted without ceasing, pray without ceasing."

~Charles Spurgeon

What is Prayer?

|incense|
Psalm 141:2 (NKJV) "Let my prayer be set before you *as* incense, the lifting up of my hands *as* the evening sacrifice."

|repentance| refreshing|
Acts 3:19 (NKJV) "Repent therefore and be converted, that your sins may be blotted out, so that times of refreshing may come from the presence of the Lord."

|abandonment|
1 Peter 5:7 (NKJV) "casting all your care upon Him, for He cares for you".

| dependence|
Psalm 116:2 (NKJV) "Because He has inclined His ear to me, Therefore I will call *upon Him* as long as I live."

|presence| lovingkindness|

Psalm 42:8 (NKJV) "The LORD will command His lovingkindness in the daytime, And in the night His song *shall be* with me—A prayer to the God of my life."

|Intercession| favour|

Exodus 32:11 (NKJV) "Then Moses pleaded with the LORD his God, and said: "LORD, why does Your wrath burn hot against Your people whom You have brought out of the land of Egypt with great power and with a mighty hand?"

|pouring out your soul|

1 Samuel 1:15 (NKJV) "But Hannah answered and said, "No, my lord, I *am* a woman of sorrowful spirit. I have drunk neither wine nor intoxicating drink, but have poured out my soul before the LORD."

|draw near| trust| praise|

Psalm 73:28 (NKJV) "But *it is* good for me to draw near to God; I have put my trust in the Lord GOD, that I may declare all Your works."

|honor|

Ephesians 3:14 (NKJV) "For this reason I bow my knees to the Father of our Lord Jesus Christ[a]."

<u>Purpose of prayer</u>

| enlightenment | knowledge |inheritance|
Ephesians 1:18 (NKJV). "the eyes of your understanding[a] being enlightened; that you may know what is the hope of His calling, what are the riches of the glory of His inheritance in the saints."

| healing| deliverance|.
James 5:13 (NKJV) "Is anyone among you suffering? Let him pray. Is anyone cheerful? Let him sing psalms."

|protection| watch|
Matthew 26:41 (NKJV) "Watch and pray, lest you enter into temptation. The spirit indeed *is* willing, but the flesh *is* weak."

|transformed| renewed| will of God|
Romans 12:2 (NKJV) "And do not be conformed to this world, but be transformed by the renewing of your mind, that you may prove what *is* that good and acceptable and perfect will of God."

|provision|
Matthew 7:11 (NKJV) "If you then, being evil, know how to give good gifts to your children, how much

more will your Father who is in heaven give good things to those who ask Him!"

|Spirit| help| intercession|
Romans 8:26-27 (NKJV) "Likewise the Spirit also helps in our weaknesses. For we do not know what we should pray for as we ought, but the Spirit Himself makes intercession for us[a] with groanings which cannot be uttered. 27 Now He who searches the hearts knows what the mind of the Spirit *is,* because He makes intercession for the saints according to *the will of* God."

|supplication| intercession| thanksgiving| leaders|.
1 Timothy 2:1-2 (NKJV) "Therefore I exhort first of all that supplications, prayers, intercessions, *and* giving of thanks be made for all men, 2 for kings and all who are in authority, that we may lead a quiet and peaceable life in all godliness and reverence."

|dream| request| revelation|
1 Kings 3:5 (NKJV) "At Gibeon the LORD appeared to Solomon in a dream by night; and God said, "Ask! What shall I give you?"

|caution| watchful|
1 Peter 4:7 (NKJV) "But the end of all things is at hand; therefore be serious and watchful in your prayers."

|ask|
James 4:2 (NKJV) "You lust and do not have. You murder and covet and cannot obtain. You fight and war. Yet[a] you do not have because you do not ask."

|ask| provision| Spirit|
Luke 11:13 (NKJV) " If you then, being evil, know how to give good gifts to your children, how much more will *your* heavenly Father give the Holy Spirit to those who ask Him!"

|love| bless|
Matthew 5:44 (NKJV) "But I say to you, love your enemies, bless those who curse you, do good to those who hate you, and pray for those who spitefully use you and persecute you,[a]"

|blessing| fasting| commissioning|
Acts 13:2-3 (NKJV) "As they ministered to the Lord and fasted, the Holy Spirit said, "Now separate to Me Barnabas and Saul for the work to which I have called

them." ³ Then, having fasted and prayed, and laid hands on them, they sent *them* away."

|divine intervention |community| intercession|
Acts 12:5 (**NKJV**) "Peter was therefore kept in prison, but constant[a] prayer was offered to God for him by the church."

|baptism| Holy Spirit| anointing|
Luke 3:21-22 (NKJV) "When all the people were baptized, it came to pass that Jesus also was baptized; and while He prayed, the heaven was opened. ²² And the Holy Spirit descended in bodily form like a dove upon Him, and a voice came from heaven which said, "You are My beloved Son; in You I am well pleased."

|inheritance| will|
Ephesians 1:11-12 (NKJV) "In Him also we have obtained an inheritance, being predestined according to the purpose of Him who works all things according to the counsel of His will, that we who first trusted in Christ should be to the praise of His glory. "

|access| boldness|
Ephesians 3:12 (NKJV) "in whom we have boldness and access with confidence through faith in Him."

|access| boldness| faith|
Hebrews 10:19-22 (NKJV) "Therefore, brethren, having boldness to enter the Holiest by the blood of Jesus, 20 by a new and living way which He consecrated for us, through the veil, that is, His flesh, 21 and *having* a High Priest over the house of God, 22 let us draw near with a true heart in full assurance of faith, having our hearts sprinkled from an evil conscience and our bodies washed with pure water."

|receive|
Luke 11:9 (NKJV) "So I say to you, ask, and it will be given to you; seek, and you will find; knock, and it will be opened to you."

|bless| remember|
Psalm 103:1-2 (NKJV) "Bless the LORD, O my soul; And all that is within me, *bless* His holy name! 2 Bless the LORD, O my soul, And forget not all His benefits."

|thanksgiving| remembrance| joy|
Philippians 1:3-4 (NKJV) "I thank my God upon every remembrance of you, always in every prayer of mine making request for you all with joy."

|revelation| seek|
Proverbs 25:2 (NKJV) "*It is* the glory of God to conceal a matter, But the glory of kings *is* to search out a matter."

|faith| healing |confession| forgiveness |effective| results|

James 5:14-16 (NKJV) "Is anyone among you sick? Let him call for the elders of the church, and let them pray over him, anointing him with oil in the name of the Lord. [15] And the prayer of faith will save the sick, and the Lord will raise him up. And if he has committed sins, he will be forgiven. [16] Confess *your* trespasses[a] to one another, and pray for one another, that you may be healed. The effective, fervent prayer of a righteous man avails much."

|miracles| results|

James 5:17-18 (NKJV) "Elijah was a man with a nature like ours, and he prayed earnestly that it would not rain; and it did not rain on the land for three years and six months. [18] And he prayed again, and the heaven gave rain, and the earth produced its fruit."

|strength| refreshment|

Isaiah 30:15 (NKJV) For thus says the Lord GOD, the Holy One of Israel: "In returning and rest you shall be saved; In quietness and confidence shall be your strength." But you would not,"

|confidence| deliverance|
Philippians 1:19 (NKJV) "For I know that this will turn out for my deliverance through your prayer and the supply of the Spirit of Jesus Christ,"

|thanksgiving |miracles| multiplication| heaven| storehouse|
Luke 9:16-17 (NKJV) "Then He took the five loaves and the two fish, and looking up to heaven, He blessed and broke them, and gave *them* to the disciples to set before the multitude. [17] So they all ate and were filled, and twelve baskets of the leftover fragments were taken up by them."

|benefits| blessing| intercession|
Job 42:10 (NKJV) "And the LORD restored Job's losses[a] when he prayed for his friends. Indeed the LORD gave Job twice as much as he had before."

|help| salvation| peace| guidance|
Psalm 107:28-30 (NKJV) "Then they cry out to the LORD in their trouble, And He brings them out of their distresses. [29] He calms the storm, So that its waves are still. [30] Then they are glad because they are quiet; So He guides them to their desired haven. "

|ask | provision|
Matthew 7:7 (NKJV) "Ask, and it will be given to you; seek, and you will find; knock, and it will be opened to you."

|prayer| fasting|
Mark 9:29 (NKJV) "So He said to them, "This kind can come out by nothing but prayer and fasting.""[a]

|miracles| life|
Acts 9:40 (NKJV) "But Peter put them all out, and knelt down and prayed. And turning to the body he said, "Tabitha, arise." And she opened her eyes, and when she saw Peter she sat up."

|ask |receive| wisdom|
James 1:5 (NKJV) "If any of you lacks wisdom, let him ask of God, who gives to all liberally and without reproach, and it will be given to him."

|faith| speak| possible|
Matthew 17:20 (NKJV) "So Jesus said to them, "Because of your unbelief;[a] for assuredly, I say to you, if you have faith as a mustard seed, you will say to this mountain, 'Move from here to there,' and it will move; and nothing will be impossible for you.""

|warfare| strongholds| might| victory|

2 Corinthians 10:4-5 (NKJV) "For the weapons of our warfare *are* not carnal but mighty in God for pulling down strongholds, [5] casting down arguments and every high thing that exalts itself against the knowledge of God, bringing every thought into captivity to the obedience of Christ, "

|supplication| victory|

Psalm 6:9-10 (NKJV) "The LORD has heard my Supplication; The LORD will receive my prayer. [10] Let all my enemies be ashamed and greatly troubled; Let them turn back *and* be ashamed suddenly. "

|abide| ask| receive|

John 15:7 (NKJV) " If you abide in Me, and My words abide in you, you will[a] ask what you desire, and it shall be done for you."

|receive| obedience|

1 John 3:22 (NKJV) " And whatever we ask we receive from Him, because we keep His commandments and do those things that are pleasing in His sight."

|revelation|
Jeremiah 33:3 (NKJV) "Call to Me, and I will answer you, and show you great and mighty things, which you do not know."

|praise| worship| deliverance| miracle|
Acts 16:25-26 (NKJV) "But at midnight Paul and Silas were praying and singing hymns to God, and the prisoners were listening to them. [26] Suddenly there was a great earthquake, so that the foundations of the prison were shaken; and immediately all the doors were opened and everyone's chains were loosed."

|Possible| might|
Luke 1:37 (NKJV) "For with God nothing will be impossible."

|Possible| might|
Mark 10:27 (NKJV) "But Jesus looked at them and said, "With men *it is* impossible, but not with God; for with God all things are possible."

|revelation| relationship| prophecy|
Amos 3:7 (NKJV) "Surely the Lord God does nothing, Unless He reveals His secret to His servants the prophets."

|strength| abide| rest|

Isaiah 40:31 (NKJV) "But those who wait on the Lᴏʀᴅ shall renew *their* strength; They shall mount up with wings like eagles, They shall run and not be weary, They shall walk and not faint."

|fasting| deliverance| favour| protection| salvation| faith| victory|

Daniel 6:18-24 (NKJV) "Now the king went to his palace and spent the night fasting; and no musicians[a] were brought before him. Also his sleep went from him. ¹⁹ Then the king arose very early in the morning and went in haste to the den of lions. ²⁰ And when he came to the den, he cried out with a lamenting voice to Daniel. The king spoke, saying to Daniel, "Daniel, servant of the living God, has your God, whom you serve continually, been able to deliver you from the lions?" ²¹ Then Daniel said to the king, "O king, live forever! ²² My God sent His angel and shut the lions' mouths, so that they have not hurt me, because I was found innocent before Him; and also, O king, I have done no wrong before you." ²³ Now the king was exceedingly glad for him, and commanded that they should take Daniel up out of the den. So Daniel was taken up out of the den, and no injury whatever was found on him, because he believed in his God. ²⁴ And the king gave the command, and they brought those men who had accused Daniel, and they cast *them* into the den of lions—them, their children, and their wives; and the lions overpowered them, and broke all their bones in pieces before they ever came to the bottom of the den."

<u>Response to prayer</u>

|listen| hear| give|
1 John 5:14-15 (NKJV), "Now this is the confidence that we have in Him, that if we ask anything according to His will, He hears us. [15] And if we know that He hears us, whatever we ask, we know that we have the petitions that we have asked of Him. "

|listen| hear| forgive|
2 Chronicles 6:21 (NKJV), "And may You hear the supplications of Your servant and of Your people Israel, when they pray toward this place. Hear from heaven Your dwelling place, and when You hear, forgive. "

|healing| deliverance| salvation|
2 Chronicles 7:14 (NKJV), " if My people who are called by My name will humble themselves, and pray and seek My face, and turn from their wicked ways, then I will hear from heaven, and will forgive their sin and heal their land. "

|believe|
Mark 11:24 (NKJV), "Therefore I say to you, whatever things you ask when you pray, believe that you receive *them*, and you will have *them*."

|hope| reveal| abandon| deliverance|
Jeremiah 29:11-15 (NKJV), "For I know the thoughts that I think toward you, says the LORD, thoughts of peace and not of evil, to give you a future and a hope. ¹² Then you will call upon Me and go and pray to Me, and I will listen to you. ¹³ And you will seek Me and find *Me,* when you search for Me with all your heart. ¹⁴ I will be found by you, says the LORD, and I will bring you back from your captivity; I will gather you from all the nations and from all the places where I have driven you, says the LORD, and I will bring you to the place from which I cause you to be carried away captive. ¹⁵ Because you have said, "The LORD has raised up prophets for us in Babylon,"

|hear|
Job 22:27 (NKJV), "You will make your prayer to Him, He will hear you, And you will pay your vows."

|righteousness| delight|
Proverbs 15:8 (NKJV), "The sacrifice of the wicked *is* an abomination to the LORD, But the prayer of the upright *is* His delight."

|mercy|

Psalm 4:1 (NKJV), "Hear me when I call, O God of my righteousness! You have relieved me in *my* distress; Have mercy on me, and hear my prayer. "

|consecration|

Psalm 4:3 (NKJV), "But know that the LORD has set apart[a] for Himself him who is godly; The LORD will hear when I call to Him."

|sincerity|

Psalm 145:18 (NKJV), "The LORD *is* near to all who call upon Him, To all who call upon Him in truth."

|Righteous| response|

Proverbs 15:29 (NKJV), "The LORD *is* far from the wicked, But He hears the prayer of the righteous."

|forgiveness| faithful|

1 John 1:9 (NKJV), "If we confess our sins, He is faithful and just to forgive us *our* sins and to cleanse us from all unrighteousness."

|meditation| consider|

Psalm 5:1-3 (NKJV), "Give ear to my words, O LORD, Consider my meditation. ² Give heed to the voice of my

cry, My King and my God, For to You I will pray.
³ My voice You shall hear in the morning, O Lᴏʀᴅ;
In the morning I will direct *it* to You, And I will look up.”

|call| hear|
Psalm 17:6 (NKJV), “I have called upon You, for You will
hear me, O God; Incline Your ear to me, *and* hear my
speech.”

|chosen| fruit|
John 15:16 (NKJV), “ You did not choose Me, but I chose
you and appointed you that you should go and bear
fruit, and *that* your fruit should remain, that whatever
you ask the Father in My name He may give you.”

|glory|
John 14:13-14 (NKJV), “And whatever you ask in My
name, that I will do, that the Father may be glorified in
the Son. ¹⁴ If you ask[a] anything in My name, I will do *it.*
”

|deliverance|
Psalm 118:5 (NKJV), “I called on the Lᴏʀᴅ in distress;
The Lᴏʀᴅ answered me *and set me* in a broad place.”

|believe|
Matthew 21:22 (NKJV), "And whatever things you ask in prayer, believing, you will receive."

|speech| meditation| acceptance|
Psalm 19:14 (NKJV), "Let the words of my mouth and the meditation of my heart. Be acceptable in Your sight, O LORD, my strength and my Redeemer. "

|supplication| faithfulness| righteousness|
Psalm 143:1 (NKJV) "Hear my prayer, O LORD, Give ear to my supplications! In Your faithfulness answer me, *And* in Your righteousness."

|thanksgiving| wisdom|
Daniel 2:23 (NKJV), "I thank You and praise You, O God of my fathers; You have given me wisdom and might, And have now made known to me what we asked of You, For You have made known to us the king's demand."

|righteousness| listening|
1 Peter 3:12 (NKJV), "For the eyes of the LORD *are* on the righteous, And His ears *are open* to their prayers; But the face of the LORD *is* against those who do evil."[a]

|sadness| healing| prophecy| chance|
2 Kings 20:5 (NKJV) "Return and tell Hezekiah the leader of My people, 'Thus says the LORD, the God of David your father: "I have heard your prayer, I have seen your tears; surely I will heal you. On the third day you shall go up to the house of the LORD.""

|intercession| healing|
Genesis 25:21 (NKJV), "Now Isaac pleaded with the LORD for his wife, because she *was* barren; and the LORD granted his plea, and Rebekah his wife conceived."

|worship|
John 9:31 (NKJV), "Now we know that God does not hear sinners; but if anyone is a worshiper of God and does His will, He hears him."

|omniscient|
Isaiah 65:24 (NKJV), "It shall come to pass. That before they call, I will answer; And while they are still speaking, I will hear."

|deliverance|
Psalm 50:15 (NKJV), "Call upon Me in the day of trouble; I will deliver you, and you shall glorify Me."

|wisdom| belief|
James 1:5-7 (NKJV), "If any of you lacks wisdom, let him ask of God, who gives to all liberally and without reproach, and it will be given to him. [6] But let him ask in faith, with no doubting, for he who doubts is like a wave of the sea driven and tossed by the wind. [7] For let not that man suppose that he will receive anything from the Lord;"

|consideration|
Psalm 102:17 (NKJV), "He shall regard the prayer of the destitute, And shall not despise their prayer."

<u>How to pray</u>

|supplications| in the spirit| watchful| perseverance|
Ephesians 6:18 (NKJV), "praying always with all prayer and supplication in the Spirit, being watchful to this end with all perseverance and supplication for all the saints,"

|thanksgiving| peace| faith|
Philippians 4:6-7 (NKJV), "Be anxious for nothing, but in everything by prayer and supplication, with thanksgiving, let your requests be made known to God; [7] and the peace of God, which surpasses all understanding, will guard your hearts and minds through Christ Jesus." |

|privacy| honesty|
Matthew 6:6-7 (NKJV), "But you, when you pray, go into your room, and when you have shut your door, pray to your Father who *is* in the secret *place*; and your Father who sees in secret will reward you openly.[a] [7] And when you pray, do not use vain repetitions as the heathen *do.* For they think that they will be heard for their many words."

|rejoicing| hopeful| patiently|
Romans 12:12 (NKJV), "rejoicing in hope, patient in tribulation, continuing steadfastly in prayer";

|Model prayer|
Matthew 6:9-13 (NKJV), "In this manner, therefore, pray: Our Father in heaven, Hallowed be Your name. [10] Your kingdom come. Your will be done On earth as *it is* in heaven. [11] Give us this day our daily bread. [12] And forgive us our debts, As we forgive our debtors. [13] And do not lead us into temptation, But deliver us from the evil one. For Yours is the kingdom and the power and the glory forever. Amen.

|solitude|
Luke 6:12 (NKJV), "Now it came to pass in those days that He went out to the mountain to pray, and continued all night in prayer to God."

|always|
Luke 18:1 (NKJV), "Then He spoke a parable to them, that men always ought to pray and not lose heart,"

|earnestly| vigilantly| with thanksgiving|
Colossians 4:2 (NKJV), "Continue earnestly in prayer, being vigilant in it with thanksgiving,"

|rejoice| always| thanksgiving|
1 Thessalonians 5:16-18 (NKJV), "Rejoice always, 17 pray without ceasing, 18 in everything give thanks; for this is the will of God in Christ Jesus for you."

|ask right|
James 4:3 (NKJV), "You ask and do not receive, because you ask amiss, that you may spend *it* on your pleasures."

|boldly| mercy|
Hebrews 4:16 (NKJV), "Let us therefore come boldly to the throne of grace, that we may obtain mercy and find grace to help in time of need."

| In faith|
James 1:6 (NKJV), "But let him ask in faith, with no doubting, for he who doubts is like a wave of the sea driven and tossed by the wind."

|bless|
Luke 6:27-28 (NKJV), "But I say to you who hear: Love your enemies, do good to those who hate you, 28 bless those who curse you, and pray for those who spitefully use you."

|praise| worship|
Acts 16:25 (NKJV), "But at midnight Paul and Silas were praying and singing hymns to God, and the prisoners were listening to them."

|thanksgiving| miracles|
Luke 9:16-17 (NKJV), "Then He took the five loaves and the two fish, and looking up to heaven, He blessed and broke them, and gave *them* to the disciples to set before the multitude. [17] So they all ate and were filled, and twelve baskets of the leftover fragments were taken up by them."

|forgiveness| clean heart|
Mark 11:25 (NKJV), "And whenever you stand praying, if you have anything against anyone, forgive him that your Father in heaven may also forgive you your trespasses."

|seek| always|
1 Chronicles 16:11 (NKJV), "Seek the LORD and His strength; Seek His face evermore!"

|thanksgiving| always|
Colossians 1:3 (NKJV), "We give thanks to the God and Father of our Lord Jesus Christ, praying always for you,"

|bless all|
Matthew 5:43-45 (NKJV), "You have heard that it was said, 'You shall love your neighbor[a] and hate your enemy.' 44 But I say to you, love your enemies, bless those who curse you, do good to those who hate you, and `pray for those who spitefully use you and persecute you,[b] 45 that you may be sons of your Father in heaven; for He makes His sun rise on the evil and on the good, and sends rain on the just and on the unjust."

|boldness| by the blood| consecration| faith|
Hebrews 10:19-22 (NKJV), "Therefore, brethren, having boldness to enter the Holiest by the blood of Jesus, 20 by a new and living way which He consecrated for us, through the veil, that is, His flesh, 21 and *having* a High Priest over the house of God, 22 let us draw near with a true heart in full assurance of faith, having our hearts sprinkled from an evil conscience and our bodies washed with pure water."

|agreement|

Matthew 18:19-20 (NKJV), "Again I say[a] to you that if two of you agree on earth concerning anything that they ask, it will be done for them by My Father in heaven.²⁰ For where two or three are gathered together in My name, I am there in the midst of them."

Father in the mighty name of Jesus, I thank you for this journey of prayer that you have started my brother and sister on. Thank you for the privilege that prayer is. Thank you for beckoning us to come and start a relationship with You of intimacy and of experiencing the fullness of the glory of the Heavenlies. Thank you Lord for Your Grace which is sufficient to teach and to guide us. Open our eyes to see as You see, open our ears to hear as You hear, open our hearts to feel as You feel, and grant us the Grace to obey. In Jesus' name. Amen

www.ingramcontent.com/pod-product-compliance
Lightning Source LLC
Chambersburg PA
CBHW051349150726
48000CB00003B/1103